# Introduction

This guide covers North Aberdeenshire: defined as the area north of Corgarff in the west and Ellon in the east. The county's western boundary runs north from Corgarff, through the Ladder Hills and up to the coast between Cullen and Portsoy. The sea bounds the county to the north and east. (Companion guides to the rest of Aberdeenshire – *Walks Aberdeen & District*, *Walks Deeside* – are also available.)

North Aberdeenshire contains a handful of large towns: the major fishing ports of Fraserburgh and Peterhead on the coast; the market towns of Huntly and Turriff inland. More typically, the area is characterised by small villages linked by a maze of single-track roads (navigation is often difficult – make sure that you always have a road map with you!). The main arterial roads are the A96, running north-west from Aberdeen, through Inverurie and Huntly; the A90, running north from Aberdeen to Peterhead and Fraserburgh; and the A98 running along the Moray Firth coast from Elgin to Fraserburgh. The area is entered from the south by a number of smaller roads crossing the hills from Deeside.

There are no high hills in the area, but there is hilly moorland in the south-west, giving some good hill walks around Strathdon *(Walks 24,28)* and Corgarff *(29,30)*. This is the eastern edge of the Grampian Mountains, and the higher walks give fine views over the county. As one moves further east and north the landscape becomes gradually flatter, though there are occasional isolated peaks: notably Tap o' Noth *(23)*, Clashmach Hill *(20)*, and Knock Hill *(17)*.

Beyond the hills, northern Aberdeenshire is essentially agricultural, making intensive use of the county's rich farmland. This does limit the potential for walking in the heart of the area, and with the exception of The Formartine & Buchan Way (a long distance path following the line of the disused Aberdeen to Fraserburgh/Peterhead railway *(8,9,10)*) and the grounds of some of the area's large houses *(12,13,14)*, the better walking in the north and east is largely found around the coast – though there are some pleasant village walks for the visitor to find which are not included in this book (the short sculpture walk in Lumsden, for example).

The coastline has enormous character. The north coast, looking onto the Moray Firth, is largely composed of cliffs interspersed with occasional sandy beaches. There is a string of fine old settlements along this coast: the little fishing villages of Sandend *(1)*, Gardenstown, Crovie *(both 4)* and Pennan *(5)*, with their characteristic rows of cottages behind the foreshore, and the larger harbour towns of Portsoy *(1)*, Banff *(2,3)* and Macduff, with the substantial port of Fraserburgh *(6)* at the eastern end of the coast. South from Fraserburgh the coast is of sand beaches and dunes *(6,7)* as far as Peterhead, beyond which there are further cliffs, including the spectacular Bullers of Buchan *(16)* – which even impressed the notoriously hard-to-please Doctor Johnson.

Visitors will also find North Aberdeenshire rich in archaeological and historic sites, with standing stones and burial cairns, hill forts,

*Portsoy Harbour (see Walk 1)*

Pictish Symbol Stones, monasteries and castles as reminders of the county's previous inhabitants.

There were once more than 200 stone circles in Aberdeenshire, though most have been destroyed and the stone reused. The arrival of the Celts around 350 BC heralded the start of the Iron Age, with new weapons, ornaments and tools. The large number of ruined hill forts (notably at Tap o' Noth *(23)* and Dunnideer *(21)*) in the area suggests that the land was considered worth protecting. The Romans invaded Britain in 55 BC, but although they reached north-east Scotland on later campaigns, there is little evidence that they managed to stay long enough to make a major impact.

Christianity arrived in the north-east around the end of the fourth century, and the most important early Christian site in northern Aberdeenshire is at Old Deer, near Mintlaw *(9)*. The current ruins are of a Cistercian abbey founded in the early 13th century, but an older, Celtic monastery existed nearby, founded by St Drostan in the 6th century. It was here that the 9th-century gospels known as the *Book of Deer* – now kept at Cambridge University – were produced.

Pictish Symbol Stones are one of the most distinctive archaeological features of the north-east. These date from between the eighth and eleventh centuries, and are stones decorated with obscure symbols, stylised animals and (on the later stones) early Christian symbols. A good example is the Picardy Stone, which can be seen near Insch *(21)*.

In the modern historical period, the area was dominated by the powerful Gordon family. At the heart of Gordon country is the small town of Huntly *(19)*, including the splendid ruin of Huntly Castle *(18)*.

North Aberdeenshire is good walking country, with a lot of interesting low level walks, plenty to see and some spectacular views from the hills and coasts. One of its great attractions is that although you are never too far away from civilization, most of the walks are very quiet, allowing you to take in the scenery and enjoy the peaceful atmosphere.

*The Picardy Stone*

# 1 Portsoy to Cullen _____ A/B

*A cliff-top coastal walk, broken by the village and beach at Sandend. In addition to the beaches there are fine rock formations, a ruined castle and two fine old ports, linked by a bus service.* **Length: 8 miles/13km** (one way); *Height Climbed:* severe undulations. **NB: This walk is unsuitable for young children and dogs unless they are kept under control at all times.**

*O.S. Sheet 29*

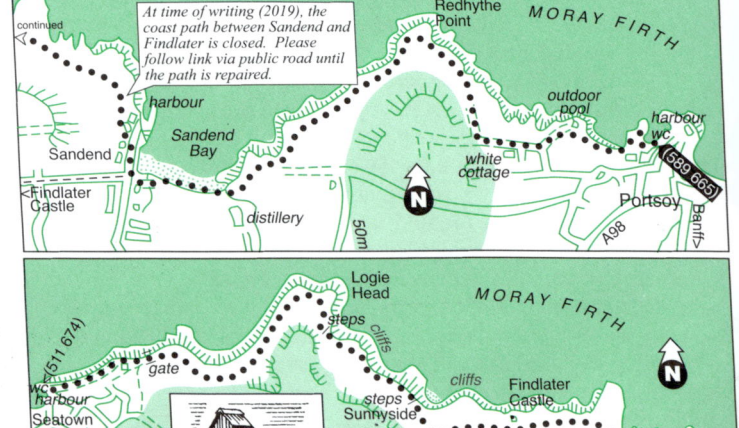

At time of writing (2019), the coast path between Sandend and Findlater is closed. Please follow link via public road until the path is repaired.

Portsoy is a small port, historically associated with the herring fishery and the export of the locally extracted 'Portsoy marble'. It is on the A98, about 7 miles west of Banff.

A coastal path runs west from Portsoy to Cullen (and beyond, but that is outwith the area covered by this guide); a stretch of coastline notable for its cliffs and stacks, for the ruin of Findlater Castle and for the little fishing village of Sandend (approximately the midway point of the walk, and a possible shorter objective).

Park by the old harbour in Portsoy (signposted from the main street) and walk down its left-hand (west) side, passing the Portsoy Marble showroom. Beyond the buildings turn left up some steps. Pass a ruined gable (on your right) and follow a rough path round to the next bay.

This path quickly runs to a dead-end, but just before this a rough path climbs steeply to the left. Follow this to the public road, where a sign points right for the Coastal Path. Follow this past a house and on along a grassy path with a fence to the right, overlooking the bay.

A tarmac road cuts right to reach the old swimming pool on the shore. Ignore this and continue on a tarmac road towards a white cottage. When the road swings left, carry straight on along a rougher track, passing in front of the cottage.

A short way beyond this the track turns half-left. Turn right at this point (marked by a green arrow) onto a grassy track by the edge of a field. This path then deteriorates before continuing around Redhythe Point as a rough footpath through grass, heather and gorse above the cliffs.

Once beyond the point Sandend comes into view ahead. The path drops slowly to reach the end of the beach, with the distillery just behind. Either walk along the beach or (if the tide is high) through the dunes behind it.

At the far end of the beach, turn inland to find a footbridge over a small burn. Cross this and turn right. It is worth continuing to the end of the road to look at the old fishermen's cottages behind the little harbour, but the path cuts left a little before this (signposted for Sunnyside Beach).

Climb up above the village and follow the narrow, grassy path along the cliff-top. This section can be overgrown in the summer, and you may wish to follow the public road as far as Findlater Castle (*see* map).

The ruined castle on its narrow headland (best observed from the viewpoint above, where there is an information board) was once a stronghold of the Ogilvie family.

Just beyond, a track heads inland (the start of the public road link with Sandend). Ignore this and continue along the cliff-top path, which eventually swings right to descend to the sands of Sunnyside Beach. The path runs through the grassland behind the beach (this can be overgrown in summer), backed by cliffs and giving fine views of the dramatic rock formations along the shore.

Beyond the far end of the beach the path climbs a splendid flight of stone steps (marked by a handsome monument to their builder, Tony Heatherington) and continues around Logie Head.

Once past the head the path runs through low ground behind a bay. You reach a metal gate, beyond which the path becomes a track then quickly splits. Keep right here, by the shore. The track rounds the last headland before Cullen and joins the road to the harbour. Beyond this you can see the cottages of Seatown (once home to Cullen's fishermen) with the disused rail viaduct – such a feature of the town – beyond.

# 2 Banff to Whitehills_____C

*This is not a walk for the solitary – it runs from a small but thriving town, along a popular beach and past a busy caravan site – but it is full of interest with great sea views.* **Length: 3 miles/5km** (one way); *Height Climbed:* negligible.

*O.S. Sheet 29*

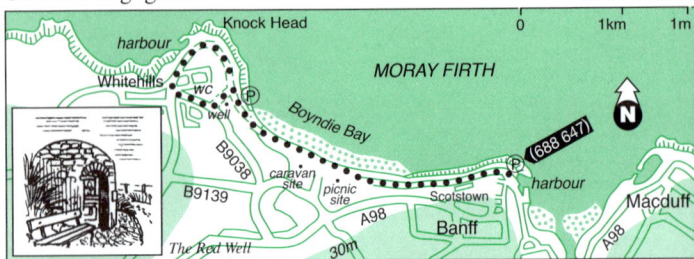

Banff is noted for the execution of James Macpherson: the Scottish Robin Hood, immortalised in the song 'Macpherson's Rant' or 'Macpherson's Lament'. His reprieve was on its way, 'coming o'er the Brig of Banff', but 'they put the clock a quarter before' and hanged him early, before it could arrive.

In Banff, follow signs for the harbour. There is ample car parking available in a landscaped car park beside the harbour.

From the car park, walk west along the coast above the sea wall following the wide tarred road. The row of old fishermen's cottages at Scotstown are beautifully maintained and face out to sea, with seats right at the edge of the wall to enjoy the view.

Continue past a large picnic area and then a caravan site which extends behind the mile-long sandy beach of Boyndie Bay. The sparkling white sands are edged with smooth boulders and then a grassy bank, and this beach can be very busy in the summer.

At the end of the caravan site a footbridge leads onto a 2m-wide path which gives easy walking towards Whitehills. There is a closed gate at the end to bar access to vehicles.

The road splits here. Keep left, passing a curious beehive structure containing a well. This has probably been in use for at least 2000 years.

The road climbs up onto the main road. Turn right here, past public toilets, and descend to the walled harbour of Whitehills. The town once had a sizeable fishing fleet, but now the harbour is filled with pleasure craft.

Turn right and walk past the adventure playground and another caravan site. The road runs round Knock Head and then returns along the coast to the fork beside the beehive well. Retrace your steps along the beach to return to Banff.

# 3 Duff House Walk                                                                      B

*This pleasant and varied walk starts and finishes at Duff House, designed by William Adam in the 1730s for William Duff, Earl of Fife. The house is well worth a visit and hosts a variety of exhibitions.*
*Length:* **6 miles/10km**; *Height Climbed:* **250ft/70m**.

*O.S. Sheet 29*

Duff House lies on the edge of Banff, close to the bridge crossing the River Deveron to Macduff. As you approach from Macduff, with the golf course on your left, there is a sign on the left for Duff House. Park in the car park to the left of the drive.

Walk on along the drive, passing to the right of a rugby pitch to reach two large gateposts marking the start of a wide shady woodland path. This leads you to the Ice House and then the Mausoleum, above a bend in the River Deveron.

Beyond the Mausoleum the track descends then passes under power lines and joins another track. Go right, and keep right at the fork just beyond. At a T-junction, with a house directly ahead of you, go left.

Follow the broad track, through farmland and woodland, to the splendid Bridge of Alvah, built in 1772. Admire the views of the river then cross the bridge and turn left (don't be tempted to go through the gate ahead). Climb gradually, passing to the left of a small pond and then Montcoffer House. Beyond this, the track jinks left then right before running straight to join the public road at a right-angled bend.

Turn left, past a cottage, then left again on a rough track. Follow this through the forest and over the hill to the Macduff Distillery. Go through the distillery and out onto the main road. Turn left, cross the bridge, and return to Duff House and the car park.

# 4 Gardenstown to Crovie  C

*Gardenstown is an attractive 18th-century fishing village on the steep slope between the headlands of Gamrie Bay. This short walk takes you round the bay to the picturesque village of Crovie. Length:* **2½ miles/4km**; *Height Climbed:* **450ft/140m**.

*O.S. Sheet 29 or 30*

Gardenstown is signposted off the B9031 Macduff to Rosehearty road, about 6 miles east of Macduff. Drive downhill, though the modern housing to the old village. Here, the amazing houses are built side by side on every available space, in the narrowest of streets. The cars, parked inches from the houses, have their wing mirrors folded in.

Turn right at the bottom of the village, towards the harbour. Go past the many small garages and park on the waste ground beyond. The path to Crovie starts here. The hillside above the path is very steep and there is some danger of rock fall, especially in very wet weather or after frost.

The path is well trodden and has clearly been used for centuries. The blackened low-lying rocks stretching out into the bay, are well-populated with screaming gulls.

The village of Crovie soon comes into view – a line of little houses, gable ends to the sea – set into the rock with the steep hillside behind. There is a narrow strip of land in front of the cottages, with wooden posts for laundry set at the edge of the sea wall. No cars are permitted, and the residents transport their goods from the car park at the foot of the road in wheelbarrows.

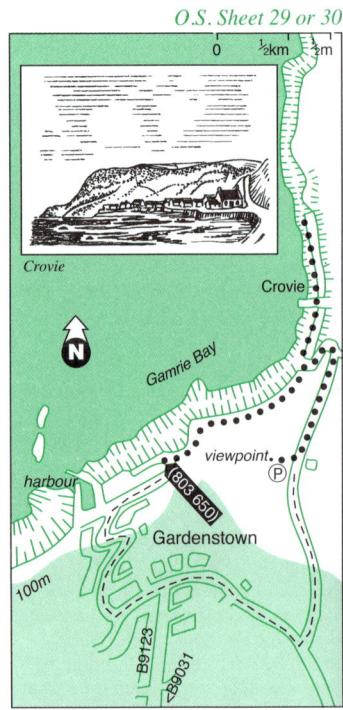

At the south end of the village a steep road climbs up the hill, and after 500m there is a car park and viewpoint. You can either return the way you came or, to complete a circuit using the road, carry on up the hill and turn right to return to the start.

# 5 Pennan to Aberdour Bay — B

*This is a fine walk through rolling farmland (grazing cattle in places), from the village of Pennan to the beach at Aberdour Bay. Length:* **4 miles/6km** (one way); *Height Climbed:* **650ft//200m**.

*O.S. Sheet 30*

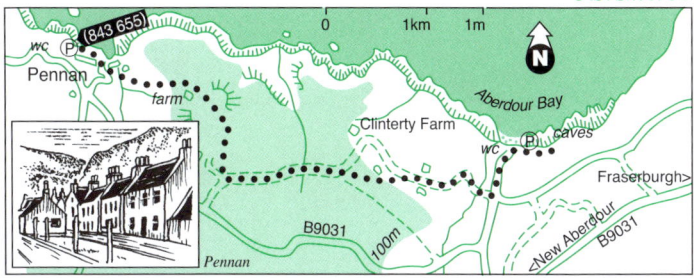

Pennan is on the north coast, 10 miles west of Fraserburgh on the B9031. It was the village used in the film *Local Hero*, and fans still visit the public telephone box featured in the film.

Drive down the steep road into the village and along the front to the car park, where there are also public toilets. Walk back along the shore in front of the attractive white houses and take the path which climbs steeply above the small harbour. It is signposted, but the sign is not obvious until you are on the path. Please keep dogs under control.

Where the slope eases go through a gate and continue climbing towards a derelict farm at the top of the hill. The path is a bit indistinct (and can be muddy), but simply follow the line of the fence. Go over a stile and round the side of the farm buildings on to a broad track. Turn right along the track and continue uphill. After about 800m the track curves to the right, but for this route follow a signpost straight ahead through a gate and along a grassy and overgrown track.

The overgrown track soon joins a surfaced road. About 100m along the road, take a signposted grass path, also overgrown, which leads back at an acute angle on the left.

Follow this for a mile/1.6km, by-passing Clinterty Farm and rejoining a good track beyond it (note the good views of Aberdour Bay ahead). Go round a sharp zig-zag then join the public road. Turn left to the car park, beach and caves of Aberdour Bay.

From the car park, follow the path east along the coast, past St Drostan's Well and then over a low rise and down to the next bay. At low tide it is possible to make your way back round the shore (**NB:** be very careful when judging the tide here), over the slabby rocks, through huge sea arches. If you take a torch, you can look in some of the caves.

# 6 Fraserburgh Bay — C

*An easy beach walk across wide sands backed by an area of dunes.*
*The path links a busy fishing harbour with a peaceful nature reserve.*
**Length: 2½ miles/4km** (one way); **Height Climbed:** none.   *O.S. Sheet 30*

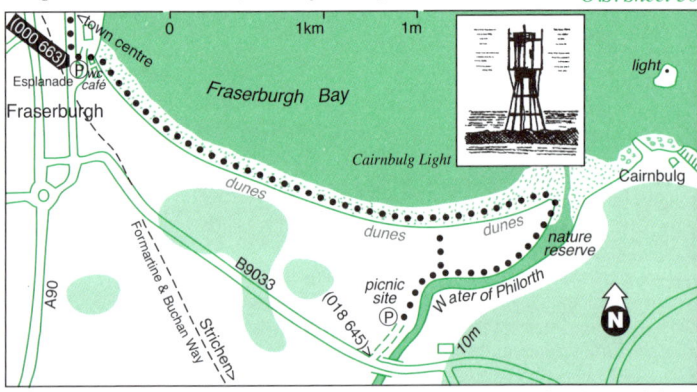

Fraserburgh is a tough working port on the windswept north-eastern point of Aberdeenshire. Its busy harbour is one of the largest white fish ports in Britain. The town is also home to the Museum of Scottish Lighthouses. To the east of the town is Fraserburgh Bay, with its splendid beach and dunes (for a longer beach walk, *see* Walk 7).

Start walking from the harbour, heading south to reach the Esplanade at the northern end of the beach (there is a car park here). Drop down to the beach and start walking around the bay (if the tide is high, it is possible to walk through the dunes). Looking ahead, you will see the headland of Cairnbulg Point, beyond the sands, with its light on an offshore skerry. The linked villages of Cairnbulg and Inverallochy are just beyond the point.

The route could not be more simple: just keep walking until you reach the Water of Philorth then cut inland by the side of the river.

The tidal area at the mouth of the river is now a small Nature Reserve, of particular interest for its dunes and reed beds. The area is attractive to waterfowl and waders.

A duckboard path cuts off this path, through the dunes and back to the beach (*see* map), making a possible loop. Alternatively, there is a car park and picnic site at the reserve.

**NB:** to reach the reserve by car, head east from Fraserburgh on the B9033. The Nature Reserve is signposted to the left of the road after 2 miles.

# 7 St Combs to Rattray Head _____ B

*An enjoyable coast walk leading to a glorious, mostly deserted beach.*
*Length:* **5 miles/8km** (one way); *Height Climbed:* none.    O.S. Sheet 30

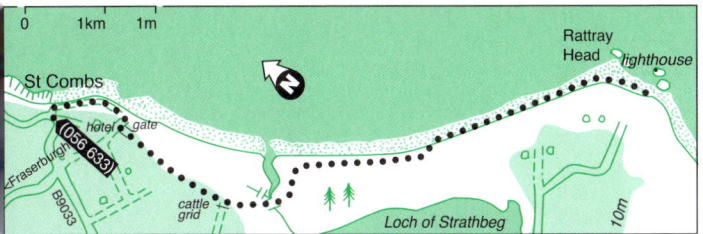

Drive south from Fraserburgh for 4 miles on the B9033 coast road then turn off to St Combs. The road becomes the main street. Follow this to its end, where it turns sharp right to a hotel. Go left here, down Church Street. Almost immediately, you pass a cemetery to your right, containing the ruins of St Columb's Church. Shortly beyond, an unmarked track heads off to the right.

Follow this path as it doubles back through the grassland behind the beach. Level with the last of the buildings up to your right you pass a concrete slipway, just beyond which a grassy path heads right to join a clear track. Turn right along this, away from the shore. Just before the track becomes a metalled road there is a gate to your left. Go through this.

Beyond the gate, keep walking on a grassy path with a fence to your right and fields beyond. The path passes through two gates then climbs gently until a track (with a cattle-grid at its end) heads off to your right.

The path now edges left, away from the fence, crosses the low watershed and descends to a bridge across a burn (there are two bridges; cross the second, larger one).

Once across the bridge, turn left. After 200 paces the path cuts right, round the base of a small sandy hillock, and sets off across a flat area between two lines of dunes. Continue until you see a sandy path rising over the dunes to your left.

Follow the path over the dunes – looking back inland you get excellent views of the RSPB sanctuary on the Loch of Strathbeg. The path leads down to a beautiful stretch of beach, broken only by the burn you crossed earlier. (**NB:** Take note of the point where path joins the beach – it will not be easy to find on the way back.)

From here, it is a straightforward, pleasant walk along the beach to the lighthouse. Near Rattray Head the beach becomes rockier, with clumps of seaweed washed up on the shore. The lighthouse itself is offshore at anything but the lowest tides.

Return by the same route.

# The Formartine & Buchan Way

*The Formartine and Buchan Way is a long distance footpath, cycleway and bridleway. It follows a disused railway line north from Dyce (near Aberdeen), through Ellon to Maud (see 'Walks Aberdeen' for Dyce to Ellon section). Here the route splits, with paths heading off to Peterhead and Fraserburgh.*

*The origin of the path dictates its character: flat, occasionally monotonous, but always clear. The total length of the path is 53 miles/86km. Along the way it passes various places of interest and runs through some fine countryside.*

*The following three entries describe sections of the path which are of particular interest.*

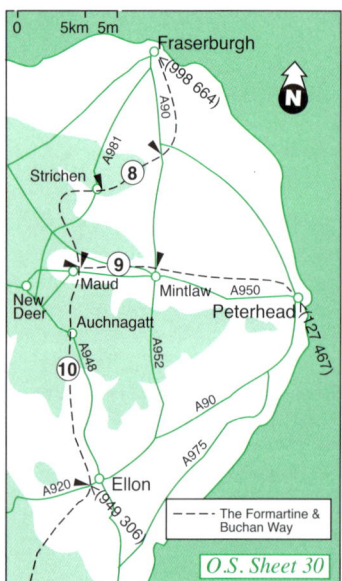

## 8 White Horse Walk, Strichen _____ C

***Part of The Formartine and Buchan Way:*** *running from Strichen, around Mormond Hill and on to meet the A952 Mintlaw to Fraserburgh road. You will have to arrange transport at the far end or retrace your steps.* **Length: 5 miles/8km** *(one way); **Height Climbed:** negligible.*

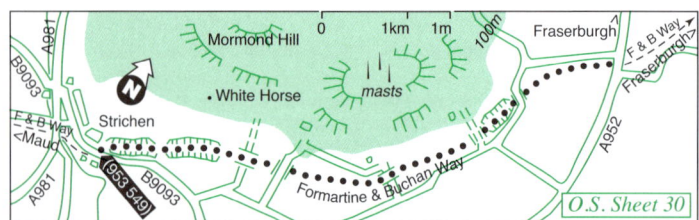

Follow the directions for the start of Walk 11, but at the Mintlaw roundabout take the A952 Fraserburgh road. After about 2½ miles turn left along the B9093 for Strichen.

Park in Strichen then walk back to the edge of the town to join the signposted track. The walking on the Way is easy and there are unobstructed views of the Buchan countryside. Mormond Hill, with its famous White Horse, dominates the northern skyline. The image of the horse – cut into the hillside and filled with white quartz – is a memorial to Sergeant James Hutcheon, who gifted his mount to Captain Fraser of Strichen at the height of battle against the French near Gilzen in Holland in 1794. The sergeant was killed before he could find a mount.

Mormond Hill is also the site of a huge collection of radar and telecommunication masts, which makes an odd contrast with the quiet path.

As you round the hill, the view opens up to the north, where Fraserburgh and the North Sea lie beyond the rolling farmland. This section of the walk ends at the junction with the A952 (it is a further 6 miles/10km to Fraserburgh).

## 9 Maud to Mintlaw _____ C

***Part of The Formartine and Buchan Way:*** *easy walking through peaceful countryside with a rich history. Possible visit to Abbey of Deer.* ***Length:*** **5 miles/8km** (one way); *Height Climbed:* negligible.

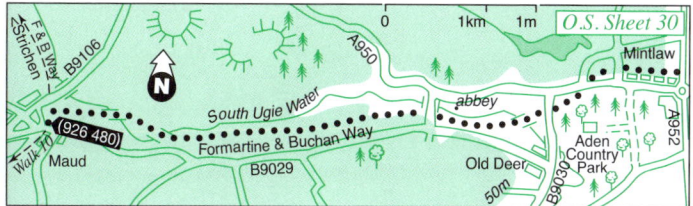

Follow the directions for the start of Walk 11, but after the Mintlaw roundabout continue along the A950 for another 4 miles then turn left down the B9106 to Maud. This quiet village was once a busy railway junction; the station closed in 1979.

Park opposite the Station Hotel, walk under the bridge and follow signs for the cycle path and walkway. Take the Mintlaw route, with open views of the countryside and of the South Ugie Water by the track. About 2 miles/3km from Maud on your right you will see Aikey Brae, where Edward Bruce, brother of Robert, defeated the Earl of Buchan in 1308.

A little further on you come to a small road. Turn left here then turn right at the main road to reach the entrance to the fine ruins of the Abbey of Deer – a Cistercian abbey founded in 1219. This ancient site, originally dedicated to St Drostan, is famous for the Book of Deer: a gospel book dating from the tenth century, now in University Library, Cambridge.

Retrace your steps to the railway line and continue towards Mintlaw. Pass a sign on your right for the village of Old Deer (only five minute walk, if you fancy a diversion) and continue to the main road. You can stay on the path for the last 1¼ miles/2km to Mintlaw or go along the main road and turn right into Aden Country Park (*see* Walk 15).

## 10 Maud to Ellon _____ B/C

***Part of The Formartine and Buchan Way:*** *running through pleasant, rolling farmland. Length:* **11 miles/17km**; *Height Climbed:* negligible.

From the centre of the village of Maud (between the Station Hotel and the Post Office) go down through a passage under the railway line, turn sharply left and then cut back up a ramp onto the line, heading towards the old Station. This is signposted to Auchnagatt (4 miles).

The old railway track leads past the station and slightly uphill. The path (always a good walking surface) passes through rich agricultural land and lightly wooded sections on the way to Auchnagatt.

Approaching the village the track stops suddenly. Take a left across the small bridge if you want to stop for refreshments at the hotel, or cross the main road on your right, continue along the road for about 10 metres and rejoin the route as it cuts off to the right. The path is signposted for Ellon.

The walk continues, ascending gently through the countryside, before descending to Ellon. The track is a little less well maintained in the downhill section before the final

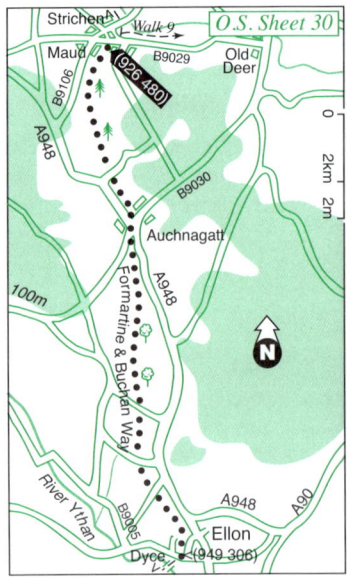

approach to Ellon: drainage problems have led to a small stream running down part of the track, so be prepared to get a bit muddy if the weather has been wet.

## 11 Forest of Deer                                                                 B

*This is a very popular local walk, half through forest and half on the edge of the forest, with sweeping views of the Buchan countryside.*
*Length:* **5 miles/8km**; *Height Climbed:* **160ft/50m**.

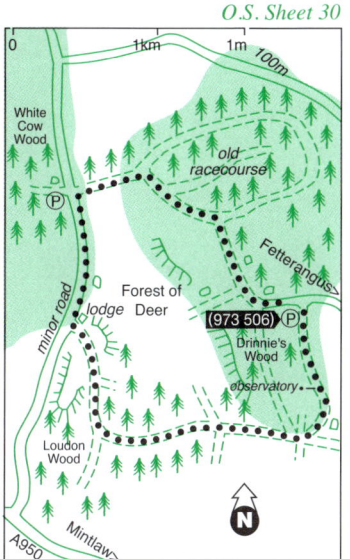

*O.S. Sheet 30*

From Peterhead, drive west on the A950. After 9 miles you pass the roundabout in the village of Mintlaw. Continue west for about a mile beyond then turn right onto the road for Fetterangus. After a mile turn left at signs for Den o' Howie and a forestry car park. Drinnie's Wood car park is a short way along the road.

Walk along the forestry road from the car park till you see a break in the trees on your right with a path leading to the restored observatory, built in 1845 by Admiral George Ferguson, 5th Laird of Pitfour. This is only open during the summer months but is well worth a visit for the fine views.

Return to the forestry road and continue to a T-junction. Turn right. Almost immediately there is a four-way junction. Keep straight on, then go left at the fork immediately beyond. Continue along the clear track, ignoring all side paths.

The route descends with open fields on the left and then climbs again as you enter Loudon Wood. Keep to the main path, which turns north until you emerge at Auchmachar Lodge on a minor road.

Turn right here and climb gently for half a mile/0.8km, enjoying the open views, till you reach the White Cow Wood car park on your left.

Just opposite the car park a track starts, signposted for Louden Wood Stone Circle. This track descends then rises steeply to reach a T-junction with a curving track on the edge of a plantation. Turn right. These tracks were part of the 4½ mile racecourse which the Admiral built to exercise his large stable of horses.

At the next junction turn right, leaving the trees and continuing between open fields till the path is tarred. Continue along this road, round a left bend, past the cluster of houses, until you return to your starting point on the right.

# Walks North Aberdeenshire

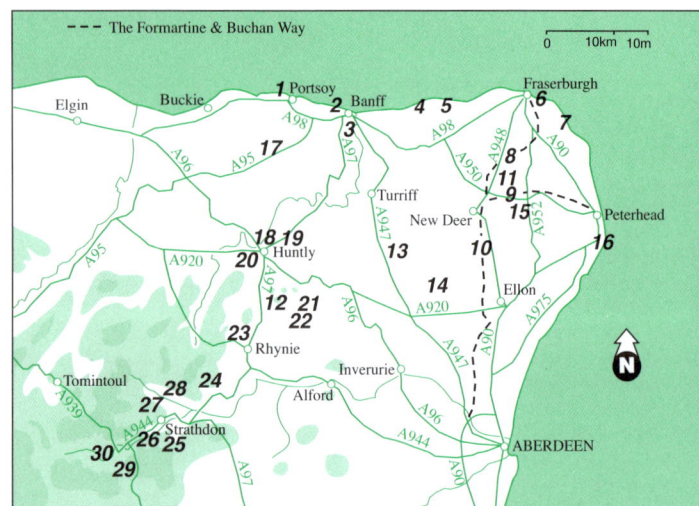

## Grades

**A** ...... Full walking equipment required

**B** ...... Strong walking footwear and waterproof clothing required

**C** ...... Comfortable walking footwear recommended

**[B/C**, etc ...... Split grades refer either to multiple route titles or to the fact that the single route described can be walked either in its entirety or in shorter, less gruelling sections.**]**

**NB:** Assume each walk increases at least one grade in winter conditions. Hill routes can become treacherous.

— www.pocketwalks.com —

**Published by:** Hallewell Publications, Scotland
**Printed by:** Barr Printers, Glenrothes

*While every care has been taken in the preparation of this guide, the publishers cannot accept responsibility for any loss, damage or injury resulting from its use.*

# Walks North Aberdeenshire

| walk | grade |
|---|---|
| 1 Portsoy to Cullen | A/B |
| 2 Banff to Whitehills | C |
| 3 Duff House Walk | B |
| 4 Gardenstown to Crovie | C |
| 5 Pennan to Aberdour Bay | B |
| 6 Fraserburgh Bay | C |
| 7 St Combs to Rattray Head | B |
| *The Formartine & Buchan Way:* | |
| 8 White Horse Walk, Strichen | C |
| 9 Maud to Mintlaw | C |
| 10 Maud to Ellon | B/C |
| 11 Forest of Deer | B |
| 12 Leith Hall | C |
| 13 Fyvie Castle | C |
| 14 Haddo House | C |
| 15 Aden Country Park | C |
| 16 Bullers of Buchan | C |
| 17 Knock Hill | B |
| 18 Huntly Castle | C |
| 19 Forest Walks around Huntly | B/C |
| 20 Clashmach Hill | B |
| 21 Dunnideer Fort | C |
| 22 Hill of Christskirk | B |
| 23 Tap o' Noth | B |
| 24 Glen Buchat | A |
| 25 Bunzeach Trail | B |
| 26 Poldullie Bridge | C |
| 27 Bellabeg to Roughpark | C |
| 28 Ben Newe | B |
| 29 Corgarff Military Road | B |
| 30 Corgarff | B |

# 12 Leith Hall / 13 Fyvie Castle / 14 Haddo House / 15 Aden Country Park ———————————— all C

*North Aberdeenshire has a number of fine old houses and castles with extensive grounds open to the public. The four described here all provide pleasant parkland and woodland walking. (See also Walk 3).*

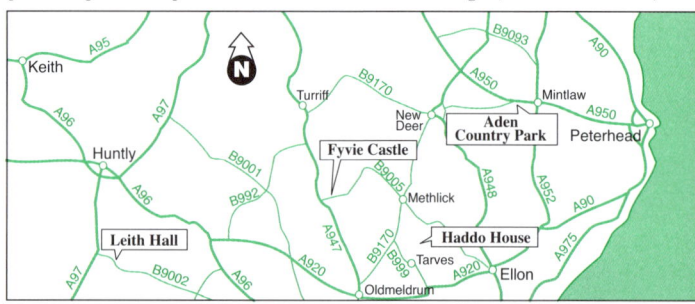

**Walk 12) Leith Hall** (NTS): *House, parkland/woodland walks, garden*

To reach Leith Hall, drive 5 miles south from Huntly on the A97, then turn east on the B9002 road for Inverurie. After 1½ miles the entrance to the Hall appears to the left. (Fee for parking).

Leith Hall is an elegant white-harled quadrangle, built in stages for the Leith family over the 17th and 18th centuries. It was gifted to the National Trust for Scotland in 1945.

In addition to the house and a fine garden, there are three signposted walks laid out through the surrounding parkland and woodland. These range from half a mile/0.8km to 1½ miles/2.4km. The shortest walk – the Pond Walk – is suitable for wheelchairs; the Craigfall Trail leads to a viewpoint overlooking the Hall.

**Walk 13) Fyvie Castle** (NTS): *House, lochside walk, garden*

Fyvie is just off the A947 between Aberdeen and Banff. If driving from Aberdeen, turn right into the village of Fyvie (signposted to the Castle), cross the River Ythan, then take a left turn (signposted) to reach the car park (parking charge).

Fyvie Castle is one of the great baronial structures in Scotland: a mass of towers made complex by its piecemeal construction over a long period, from the 12th century to the 19th. It also contains a fine collection of paintings. The building – plus grounds of 118 acres/48ha – was bought by the National Trust for Scotland in 1984.

A 1¼ mile/2km walk around the narrow Loch of Fyvie starts from the car park. It is marked by yellow arrows, which lead you through an ornamental gateway, through some gardens, and then to the waterside. Follow the path as it runs clockwise around the loch.

**Walk 14) Haddo House** (NTS/Aberdeenshire Council): *House, parkland/lochside walks*

To reach Haddo House and the surrounding Country Park, turn off the B999 Methlick-Pitmedden road just east of Tarves and follow the signs.

The house is in the Palladian style, and was designed for William, 2nd Earl of Aberdeen, by William Adam in the early 18th century. The house is run by the National Trust for Scotland; the surrounding Country Park by the local Council.

The grounds are a fine example of the landscaping of the period, with an ornamental lake (with bird hides), long vistas and straight rides. There are no specific walking routes laid out, but the 5 miles/8km of connected paths will suggest plenty of options. A leaflet is available from the visitor centre.

**Walk 15) Aden Country Park** (Aberdeenshire Council): *Heritage Centre/café, woodland walks*

From Mintlaw, drive west on the A950 towards Old Deer. There are signs for the Country Park on your left as you leave the village. Follow the signs for the farming museum and the main car park (parking charge).

The signposted walks (up to 4 miles/6km) begin near the farming museum: on the other side of the courtyard from the museum, behind the ranger station.

Whichever walk you do, make sure you visit the nearby Mansion House: an imposing ruin, less than 100m from the museum.

# 16 Bullers of Buchan _____C

*This is a very short, very spectacular walk passing sea cliffs and natural arches. Dr Johnson described the view as one 'which no man can see with indifference who has either sense of danger or delight in rarity'.*
*Length:* **1½ miles/2.5km** *(there and back); Height Climbed:* negligible.
**NB: High cliffs and narrow paths. Route unsuitable for small children, dogs and anyone who suffers from vertigo.**

*O.S. Sheet 30*

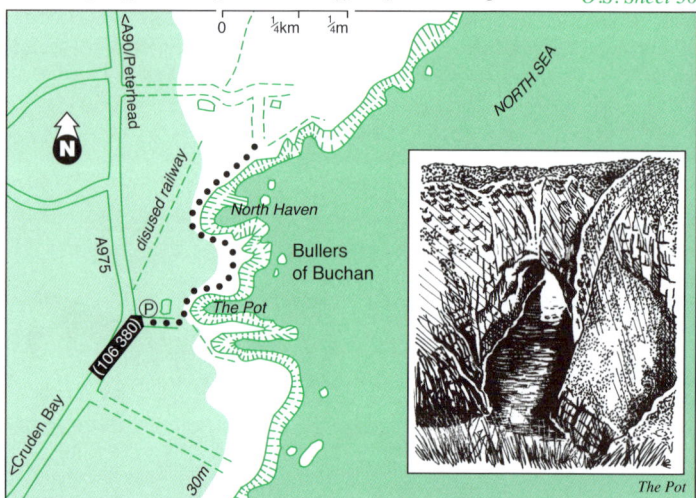

The Pot

The signposted car park for the Bullers of Buchan is 2 miles north of Cruden Bay on the A975, to the right of the road. Park in the car park and walk down past the group of cottages.

Swing left in front of the cottages to reach an information board overlooking The Pot. This is a huge collapsed sea cave that has left a hole 100ft/30m deep. The sea roars into The Pot through the old cave entrance and the spectacle is terrifying on a stormy day. The word 'bullers' is probably derived from 'boilers' – a reference to the boiling masses of foam in The Pot.

Continue on the narrow path around the headland beyond. This takes you to North Haven: a deep bay with a dramatic stack. Steps lead down to the shingle beach. Note the rusting winch, which once would have pulled boats up the beach.

Continue along the cliff tops to a turning point at the foot of a track, then return by the same route.

# 17 Knock Hill ──────────────────────────────B

*Knock Hill dominates the surrounding farmland and is visible for miles around. The path to the top is steep, uncompromising and difficult underfoot, but the views and sense of accomplishment make the ascent worthwhile. Length:* **1½ miles/2.5km** (there and back)*; Height Climbed:* **750ft/230m**.

*O.S. Sheet 29*

Follow the A95 Keith to Banff road from Keith for about 8 miles. About half a mile after the junction with the B9022, and the Glenbarry Hotel, turn left onto a tarred road, immediately after a cottage. Knock Hill is unmistakeable.

Follow this road for a little less than a mile and park on the left at a T-junction with a track. Walk a few paces to the right then turn left onto a path between disused gateposts. Walk straight up through a grassy area with trees and gorse bushes. Near the top edge of the trees there is a fence. The path goes through a gap where there used to be a gate, on to the open hill.

The path takes the direct route and is challenging. Near the summit there is a fence round the hill, but go through a gate and the summit with its trig-point is not far ahead. The views are terrific with the Moray Firth to the north and the Grampian hills and Bennachie to the south. The descent is equally demanding, so take care.

*Knock Hill, seen from the south-east*

# 18 Huntly Castle_____C

*A short walk to a splendid ruined castle, with a possible extension along the River Deveron and back through mixed woodland.* Length: up to **3 miles/5km**; *Height Climbed:* negligible.

*O.S. Sheet 29*

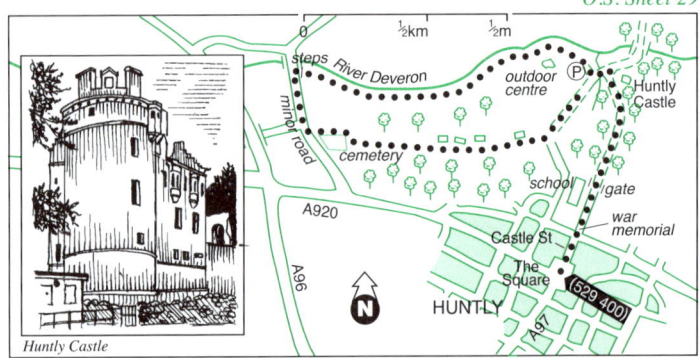

*Huntly Castle*

The handsome gridiron town of Huntly, by the junction of the Rivers Bogie and Deveron, owes its existence to the powerful Gordon family. For several centuries the family's main stronghold was Huntly Castle; now a dramatic ruin.

Park in the town square and walk down Castle Street. This leads to a junction. Cross over and continue straight ahead; past a fine war memorial then through an imposing gatehouse (part of Gordon Schools). Continue beyond along a straight driveway to the castle.

The castle began life as a motte and bailey in the 12th century, but the growing wealth and power of the warlike Gordons led to numerous extensions and rebuilds. The existing structure dates mainly from the 16th and 17th centuries and is open to the public (charge).

It is possible to return from here. If you wish to continue with the longer walk, go round the left-hand side of the castle and watch for a sign to the Nordic & Outdoor Centre. Turn left here, crossing a bridge over a burn, then go right, into a car park.

Walk to the far end of the car park and continue along a clear track by the river. Follow the riverbank, ignoring tracks and paths heading off to the left, for a little under a mile/1.6km to reach the first road bridge. Climb the steps by the bridge to join the minor road and turn left along the pavement.

Just before a cemetery turn left, at a sign for 'Meadows Plantings Walk', and follow a complex sequence of signposted paths, through woodland, back to the castle.

# 19 Forest Walks around Huntly ———————— B/C

*There are two woodland walking areas in and around Huntly. Battlehill can be reached on foot from the town; The Bin Forest has a separate car park, a short way up the A96.*

O.S. Sheet 29

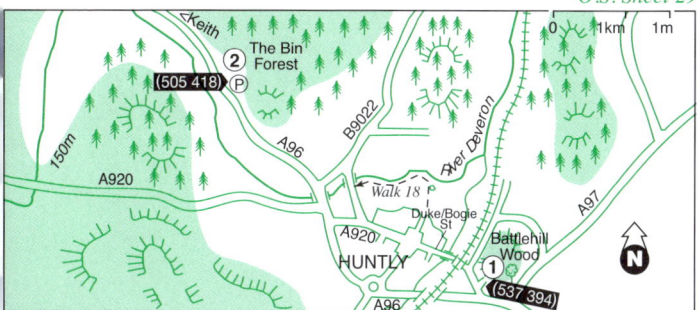

**1) Battlehill** is an area of mixed woodland, popular with local walkers, on the eastern edge of the town. To reach it from the town centre, walk (or drive – there is a small car park) along Duke Street and Bogie Street, passing under the railway bridge, then turn left at a sign for Battlehill Wood.

The easiest route is to follow the path around the edge of the wood but there are numerous paths passing over the wooded hill. A board at the start of the walk shows the options. Apart from the pleasant woodland, the hill is archaeologically interesting, with ancient burial cairns and the remains of an Iron Age fort. *Length: 1½ miles/2.3km (circuit of the wood).*

**2) The Bin Forest** *(right)* is a much larger forest area containing a number of possible routes. To reach it, drive 2 miles north of Huntly on the A96 Keith road. The car park is to the right of the road.

The Forestry Commission has laid out a variety of walks: *Lengths: 1½ miles/2.5km to 5 miles/8km.* The route up The Bin involves a climb of around 550ft/170m.

A leaflet showing the walks in detail is available in the car park.

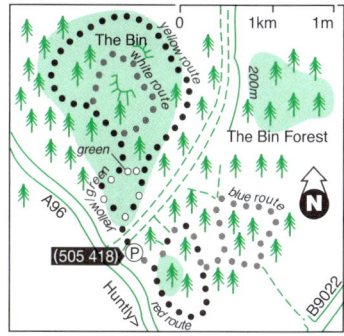

# 20 Clashmach Hill — B

*Clashmach Hill is a rounded hill just outside Huntly. It is a fine viewpoint, and it is claimed that on a good day you can see as far as the hills of Caithness. Length:* **5 miles/8km** (there and back)*; Height Climbed:* **850ft/250m**.

*O.S. Sheet 29*

Drive into Huntly from the roundabout on the A96. After 200m there is a free car park with toilets on your left.

Walk back to the roundabout and cross the A96 at the island (take care, it is a busy road). Turn right on the far side of the road to reach a minor road heading left, signposted for Tullochbeg.

Walk up the Tullochbeg road, passing Huntly Mart on your right. The road turns right, then left at a junction, and climbs quite steeply to reach a bungalow. Even from here you have a fine view of Huntly.

At the bungalow the road turns left, but you keep straight on. The clear path swings right, across the slope, then left (by a wind turbine), before climbing again, with a fence to its left. Pass through a gate in a fence to reach the open hill, then another shortly before the summit.

From the top, looking south, you can see Ben Rinnes, Tap o' Noth (Walk 23) and the distinctive top of Bennachie to the south-east. To the north, are The Bin (Walk 19) and Knock Hill (Walk 17). You may even see the Moray Firth and the hills of Caithness! Descend the same way.

*Clashmach Hill seen from Huntly (Walk 18)*

# 21 **Dunnideer Fort** / 22 **Hill of Christskirk** ——— **C/B**

*Two short hill climbs leading to good views.* **21)** *Dunnideer Hill has been fortified since prehistoric times and there is the ruin of an old tower on the summit.* Length: **1 mile/1.6km** (there and back); Height Climbed: **300ft/90m**. **22)** *Hill of Christskirk provides a longer walk to a slightly higher summit.* Length: **3 miles/5km** (there and back); Height Climbed: **550ft/170m**.

*O.S. Sheet 37*

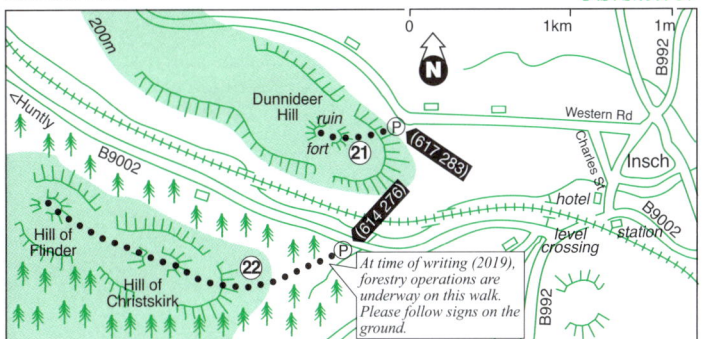

The village of Insch is about 12 miles south-east of Huntly on the A97/B9002. Approaching from that direction you will see the ruin on the top of Dunnideer Hill to the north of the road. Hill of Christskirk is opposite it to the south.

**Walk 21)** Starting from the railway station in Insch, drive past the Station Hotel, turn left up Charles Street and then left along Western Road. Just over a mile from the village centre there is a car park and information board on the left.

Go through a gate at the back of the car park and turn right up a grassy track. This goes through a second gate on the way to the summit. The path passes through the remains of Iron Age ramparts before reaching the ruins of a 13th-century castle on top of the hill.

There are fine views from the summit: south-east to Bennachie and west to Tap o' Noth (*see* Walk 23).

**Walk 22)** Drive a mile west from Insch on the B9002 and watch for a car park to the left of the road.

A sign for 'Christ's Kirk Walk' points up a ride in the trees. There are no signs beyond this, but if you keep heading uphill you will eventually climb into the open.

Once above the trees, the route to the low summit is clear. Keep straight on beyond the top if you wish to visit the lower Hill of Flinder, then return by the same route.

# 23 Tap o' Noth _____ B

*Three thousand years ago, the fort on this hill top must have been a site of some power. It dominates the countryside and the walled compound on the summit is still breathtaking.* Length: **4 miles/6km** (there and back); Height Climbed: **1000ft/300m**. *Fine views.*

O.S. Sheet 37

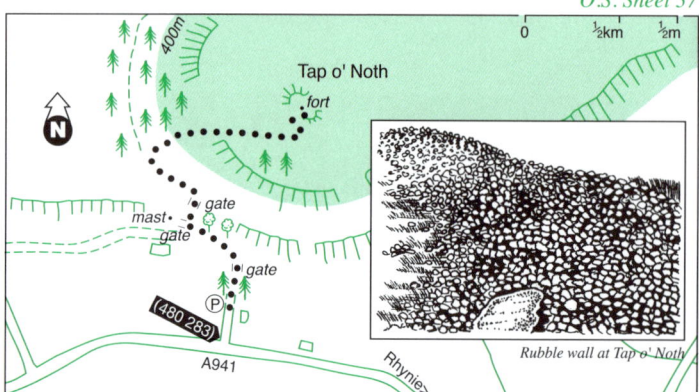

Rubble wall at Tap o' Noth

Drive to Rhynie, about 8 miles south of Huntly on the A97. From the centre of the village take the A941 Dufftown road. After 1½ miles turn right at a sign for the Tap o' Noth footpath and follow the narrow road to the car park and information board.

Turn left out of the car park and follow a broad track gently uphill. Cross a stile beside a gate (please keep dogs under control). After going through a narrow belt of trees you pass through a gate in a fence and turn left, across the slope, with the fence to your left.

You reach a gate leading to a telephone mast. Turn right on the near side and walk uphill with a fence to your left to reach another gate.

Beyond this you are on a clear path on the open hill.

There is no doubt about the route. The path climbs onto the ridge of the hill, then zig-zags up to the fort on the summit. Just short of the top there is a board explaining what can be seen in the view (which is excellent), then you go through the rubble ring and into the fort.

The size of the enclosed area is astonishing. Close to the trig point there are sections of vitrified, or melted, rock. This was probably part of the construction process, though it may have been caused by a conflagration which destroyed the fort.

Return the same way.

# 24 Glen Buchat ——————————————————————————A

*With its imposing ruined castle and quiet stream meandering through farmland and woodland, Glen Buchat is a great example of the beauty of the Aberdeenshire countryside. This walk takes you onto the ridge between Glen Buchat and Glen Kindie, and can easily be extended. Length:* **7½ miles/12km**; *Height Climbed:* **1300ft/400m**.

O.S. Sheet 37

To reach the start, drive 4 miles east from Strathdon on the A944/A97, keeping by the River Don. Just beyond the entrance to Glen Buchat Castle the Glen Buchat road heads off to the left. There is limited parking here. Walk up the minor road, passing a first farm then taking the access road to the second farm, called 'Blackhillock'. (**NB:** although this is an established walk, this is a working farm and should be treated as such.)

Follow the road up to the farm then round its right-hand side and behind a barn. Here you will find a gate. Beyond this, the path dips to cross a little burn, then climbs towards the ridge as a grassy track.

Climb to a gate, in line with the bottom of a conifer plantation to your right, then walk up the right-hand side of the field beyond to reach another gate, in line with the top of the trees. Beyond this you are on the open moor, and a track zig-zags up the slope, initially heading to the right of the rocky hillock at the end of the ridge before doubling back beneath the rocks and climbing onto the ridge.

Walk along the ridge, passing through a gate before climbing the first hill, and a second gate in the col before Meikle Firbriggs Hill. In the next dip in the ridge a track starts to your left. This is the return route, but before descending continue to the summit of Creag an Eunan ahead (from where experienced walkers can extend the route to north or west).

Return to the junction and follow the track downhill. You pass through some pleasant fields, then a metal gate, then down the access road to a house. At the end of the road, turn left along the glen road for about 2½ miles/4km to return to the start.

# 25 Bunzeach Trail / 26 Poldullie Bridge / 27 Bellabeg to Roughpark _____ B/C/C

*Three signposted walks from the village of Bellabeg.* **25)** *A complex circuit through mixed woodland on Coulick Hill. Paths are generally good, and there are possible shorter versions. Length:* up to **5 miles/8km**; *Height Climbed:* **820ft/250m**. **26)** *A short, lineal walk on a quiet minor road, leading to a picturesque old bridge. Length:* **2 miles/3km** (there and back); *Height Climbed:* negligible. **27)** *A lineal path, through mixed woodland, passing a splendid medieval motte. Length:* **1½ miles/2.4km** (there and back); *Height Climbed:* negligible.

*O.S. Sheet 37*

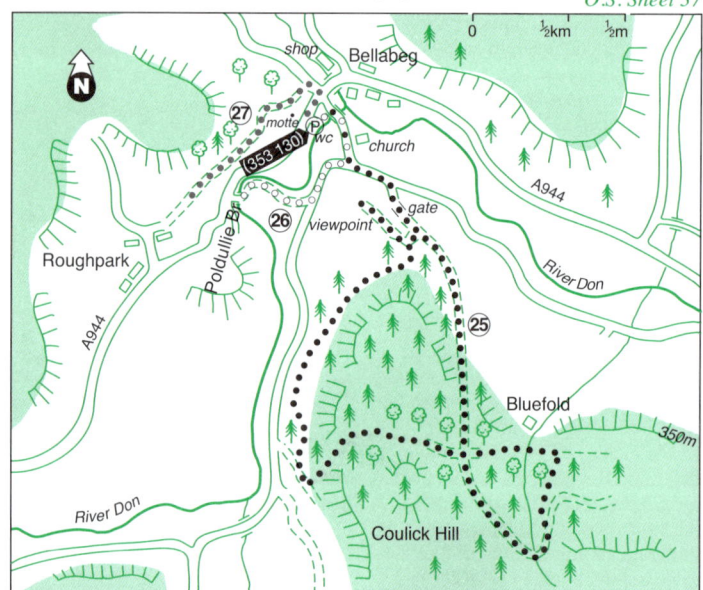

Strathdon is a beautiful stretch of the upper River Don, with a pleasant mix of farmland, woodland and low hills. The area is not well defined, and there are a number of small settlements, the largest of which is Bellabeg.

To reach Bellabeg, drive 24 miles south from Huntly on the A97/A944. Drive past the shop and over the bridge beyond. Just after you pass the war memorial (on your right) there is a car park to the left of the road.

**Walks 25 & 26)** At the back of the car park there is a board showing the routes, just beside which is a sign for the Bunzeach Trail. Follow the path indicated, by the river, to reach the bridge. Cross over and walk up past the church to reach a T-junction.

**Walk 25)** Turn left, along the road. After 200 paces a track heads off to your right, signposted for the walk. Walk past a gate and continue for a short distance to reach a junction. The track to your right is your return route (and also a shortcut to the viewpoint), but for this walk keep straight on.

The track starts up the edge of the forest, then enters the trees. After a short distance you reach a four-way junction. A turn to the right will shorten the route (*see* map), but otherwise keep straight on.

The track climbs gently to a hairpin bend. 70 paces beyond the bend go left, onto a grassy track. This leads down to a T-junction on the edge of the trees. Turn left to return to the four-way junction.

Keep straight on, climbing through beech trees then descending to a T-junction. Go right. After a few paces a post with a blue ring marks the start of a grassy path. Follow this back into the trees.

When the path swings right, watch for a waymarked path starting to your left. Follow this to the edge of the trees and turn right, with a minor road down to your left.

The path shadows the road for a while, then edges right. After a short distance it joins a field edge to the left. When the field ends the path climbs through conifers, with the remains of an old wall to the left. Before you reach the top of the climb, a post marks the start of a path to the left. Turn on to this.

The path runs a short distance through the trees to reach a ride with a fence on the far side. Go through a gate in the fence, through a narrow plantation beyond, then through a second gate to join a clear track. A turn to the left at this point leads to the viewpoint, overlooking the church. Otherwise turn right to return to the junction passed before.

**Walk 26)** Turn right and follow the quiet road over a wooded hill. As you start to descend a signposted track heads off to the right, leading down to the handsome old bridge at a wooded bend in the river.

Return by the same route.

**Walk 27)** Leave the car park and turn right along the road, then cross over to the war memorial. Near this you will see the start of a path (to the left) and a sign for Roughpark.

Follow the clear path past the grassy, moated mound of Doune of Invernochty (all that remains of a 12th-century castle) and continue, passing to the right of a pond.

The clear path runs through fine woodland. When it exits the trees there is a bench to your right, overlooking the row of houses at Roughpark. Turn back here.

# 28 Ben Newe  B

*A waymarked climb through conifer woodland leading to the summit of Ben Newe, with spectacular views over the surrounding countryside.*
*Length:* **4 miles/6km**; *Height Climbed:* **650ft/200m**.

*O.S. Sheet 37*

Drive 1½ miles east from Strathdon on the A944 and a sign to the left indicates 'Forestry walks'. Follow the road for 1300m to the second car park (Deochry car park). There is a sign for the walk at the entrance, marked by a blue arrow.

Walk up the track from the car park, passing a small lochan. Just before a second lochan the track bends half-right (blue arrow) and heads uphill through mature conifer woodland, with the remains of an old wall to the left.

*At time of writing (2019) there is forestry work being undertaken around this route. Please follow any signs on the ground.*

The track climbs obliquely across the slope to reach a hairpin bend. There is a junction here; double back to the right (blue arrow) and keep climbing.

As you go across the slope there is a fenced area to your left. When the fence ends ignore a path to the left and keep straight on along the rough track. This leads to a wide turning area, at the end of which there is a junction. Ignore the track going straight on and double back up to the left (blue arrow).

As you climb, an old track heads off to the left. Ignore this and keep right (blue arrow), through an area of semi-felled forestry. As you approach the watershed there is a split, with one track going straight on and the other heading left. Go left (arrow).

Continue across the slope until you reach the line of an old fence. You turn right here (arrow), with the fence to your left, and climb through a fringe of trees to reach the heathery hilltop with its rocky outcrops.

You will find the remains of a Celtic Holy Well to one side of the summit, but the main attraction of the walk is the view. Hills are visible in every direction, but nearer at hand you will see Glen Buchat, with its castle and the line of peaks visited by Walk 24. To the east you look down the valley of the River Don.

Return by the same route.

# 29  Corgarff Military Road _____ B

*This was part of the military road linking Fort George, on the Moray Firth, with Blairgowrie. It was built around 1750 as part of General Wade's massive road building project. Only a short stretch remains, but it gives easy access to the nearby hills.* **Length: 3 miles/5km** (one way; add **3 miles/5km** for optional hill climb); **Height Climbed: 300ft/90m** (west to east) (**1000ft/300m** including hill climb).

*O.S. Sheet 37*

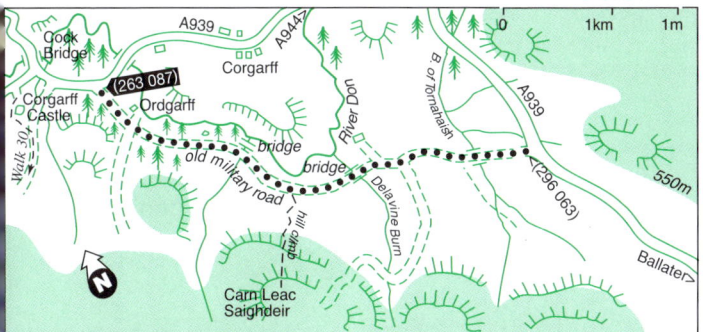

About ⅓ mile east of Corgarff Castle, on a bend in the A939, there is a sign indicating a 'public footpath by Old Military Road'. It is possible to park at the road end or in a lay-by on the right about 300m further down the track. (The other end of the track is 1½ miles south of the junction with the A944 and is similarly signposted.)

Follow the track indicated by the sign, into the conifer woodland. Just beyond the lay-by the track reaches a four-way junction by some houses at Ordgarff. Keep straight on here.

Shortly beyond a small cottage the conifers end and you reach a small burn crossed by one of the old military bridges. (The bridge is semi-collapsed and unsafe, but the burn is easy to ford). Beyond this the track climbs uphill, giving excellent views of the road stretching ahead and of the valley and hills.

Just as the track begins to descend there is a log ramp on your right, and a path zig-zags up to the summit of Carn Leac Saighdeir (699m) – a steep ascent rewarded by good views. Descend by the same route, then continue along the old road.

Carry on, crossing the splendid old military bridge over the Delavine Burn and climbing the slope on the other side. At the top the road splits. Follow the wider way to the left. This leads down to the bridge over Burn of Tornahaish, then climbs up to join the public road.

# 30 Corgarff _____ B

*Corgarff Castle is a tower house dating from the mid 16th century. It is surrounded by a star-shaped curtain wall which was added in 1748 when it became a military outpost. The walk, on clear stalking paths, starts behind the castle. Length:* **6 miles/9.5km**; *Height Climbed:* **1000ft/300m**. *NB: This is a sensitive stalking area; avoid this route in Sep/Oct, except on Sundays.*

Corgarff Castle is in the care of Historic Scotland and is open daily in summer and at weekends in winter.

Park in the castle car park and walk up towards the walled keep. Just before you reach the castle (which is worth a visit before you go further) there is a field gate to your right. Go through this (being careful to close it behind you) and walk uphill with the fence to your left. At the top of the field cross a stile and swing left on a rough path above the castle. Watch for a small path leading down to the left to join the main track, running up the glen.

This is a wide stalking path. The way is obvious, passing through a gate and then heading towards a small conifer plantation. Just before you reach the trees the track splits. Keep left, running up the side of the trees and then bending to the right and climbing towards the watershed.

Just before the watershed the track forks. Go right. The track remains clear right onto the plateau, but disappears in the rocks around the cairn on Carn Oighreag. Head straight for the cairn then continue beyond, edging left to rejoin the track. The view is spectacular, with the

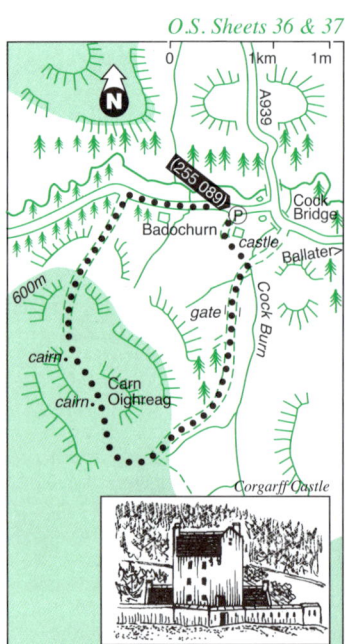

*O.S. Sheets 36 & 37*

castle below and the low, rolling hills.

The track descends gently at first, then more steeply; dropping down the heather slope to join a quiet tarred road above the River Don.

Turn right along the road to return to the castle car park.